Jasper Whitfield Snowdon

An Account of the Society of Union Scholars

Established, A.D. 1713, with the Members' Names, Rules, and Peal Book,

from the Original M.S.S. ...

Jasper Whitfield Snowdon

An Account of the Society of Union Scholars
Established, A.D. 1713, with the Members' Names, Rules, and Peal Book, from the Original M.S.S. ...

ISBN/EAN: 9783337249786

Printed in Europe, USA, Canada, Australia, Japan

Cover: Foto ©ninafisch / pixelio.de

More available books at **www.hansebooks.com**

OSBORNE M.S.S.

———:o:———

Additional M.S.S. British Museum Library,
Nos. 19368; 19370 and 19371.

———:o:———

AN ACCOUNT

OF THE

SOCIETY OF UNION SCHOLARS,

ESTABLISHED, A.D. 1713.

With the Members' Names, Rules, and Peal Book,
from the original M.S.S.,

AND AN APPENDIX

BY

JASPER W. SNOWDON and ROBERT TUKE,

OF THE

YORKSHIRE ASSOCIATION OF CHANGE RINGERS,

———

JOHN DALE AND CO., PRINTERS, BRIDGE STREET AND LEEDS ROAD,
BRADFORD.

—

1877.

BRITISH MUSEUM LIBRARY.

ADDITIONAL MANUSCRIPTS,

Vol. 19,370.

"ACCOUNT OF THE RINGING SOCIETIES
IN LONDON, BY
E. J. OSBORNE.

—:o:—

THE UNION SCHOLARS, ESTABLISHED, 1713.

—:o:—

This antique Society was established in the 13th year of the reign of Queen Anne, on the 1st of May, 1713. In the 3rd article by which the Society was regulated, it was ordered that the meetings should be held "within the City of London," what part of the city does not appear, but from the circumstance of the first peal being rung at St. Dunstan's in the East, the probability is, the meetings were held contiguous to that church. As nothing now remains (excepting the record book) to shew the exact origin of the Union Scholars' Society, it cannot now be more accurately known than by the following observations; but those who are fond of tracing marks of antiquity relating to the ringing exercise, must, I feel assured, regret the loss of knowing the true original particulars of this Company. This neglect, perhaps, may be accounted for by remarking that the ancients in this exercise were generally very dilatory and neglectful in recording the exploits of their day.

It appears that the beautiful Tower of St. Dunstan's in the East was erected in the year 1690, and the present peal of bells was cast and put up in 1702, which is evidenced by the following singular notice copied from an old newspaper, to be seen in the British Museum, called the *Post Boy*, and dated July 25th, 1702, which states that:—

> 'Whereas, Mr. Abraham Rudhall, of the city of Gloucester, bell founder, was lately employed to cast 8 bells for the Parish Church of St. Dunstan's, in London. This is to give notice that he has performed his contract to the universal satisfaction of the gentlemen of the said Parish, and in the opinion of the ablest judges has made them the best peal of bells in all England.'

The probability is that soon after these bells were put up the Union Scholars began to hold meetings and practised ringing of some kind at St. Dunstan's prior to their establishing a society. I am of opinion, as this was a city society, and from the fact of their first peal being rung there,—the first known peal upon the bells—the Union Scholars were the original parochial ringers of St. Dunstan's.

The Union Scholars had one book in which are recorded their Articles, Names and Peals. The Articles, seven in number, proclaim that every candidate must be a strictly moral character to become eligible for admission, and if approved, should pay 1s. the entrance fee, and thereby become a member. There are 181 names of members, written in bold German text, with dates, &c., shewing accurately the times of their admission and the times of appointments to the offices of Master and Stewards. A Master and two Stewards were chosen annually, and the Annual Festival was ordered to be held on the 1st of May, at some convenient place in the City of London. The book also contains an account of 36 peals (mostly plain ringing), the first of which is dated 1718, and the last 1757. There is one circumstance connected with the three first entries which calls forth some remarks and surprise, i e., the first and second peals were rung in September and

December, 1718, and the space of 18 years passed over before the next peal was rung. This can possibly be accounted for in the following manner, i e., by reason of the peal in December being the very first peal of Treble Bob that ever was rung in the kingdom—which was at the time and many years after called "Union Bob," so named in honour of the Union Scholars ringing the first peal in that method,—after ringing this peal, those members who rang it appear to have left the company, as their names (afterwards) do not appear as Union Scholars, or in fact as anything else in that way; the presumption is therefore that they joined the London Scholars, who were a most respectable ringing society and of great renown, but whether anything of consequence was ever done by these people conjointly, in the way of peals, is now unknown, and will, I expect, be for ever so, in consequence of the total loss of the London Scholars' record books. The first peal (before-mentioned) rung by the Union Scholars is called a peal of "Hick's Tripples," *—so named possibly after the person of that name who invented the method. There is no note or name of bob caller to either peal. The writings representing these two peals in 1718, are the *oldest* ringing records *upon paper* in the kingdom, and are in good condition, considering the number of years they have been written! At and after this supposed loss of members above-mentioned, the Society continued to receive new members, and went on in the usual way, yet, the fact is they appear to have been so far reduced as not to be able to ring a peal until 18 years afterwards. However, after the expiration of this period, they again began to ring peals, as frequently as other societies, to the year 1754.

In the year 1745, Mr. John Holt (the renowned author of the celebrated peal of Grandsire Triples), was admitted a member

* Mr. Osborne is not quite correct in this, it is entered as "Hick Tripples" and the "Garthornes Hic Tripples" to be found in Annable's Note Book, shew that it was in reality Grandsire with fifth place bobs, and there is every reason to suppose that the peal was identical with Garthon's peal which had been performed by the Norwich Scholars on August 26th. 1718.

of the Union Scholars, and in 1749 served the office of Master. During the time of his Mastership with this Company, he successfully accomplished his much celebrated long course peal of Grandsire Triples, which was for the first time rung at St. Margaret's, Westminster, on Sunday, July 7th, 1751, himself seated upon a chair in the steeple and conducting the same; he afterwards composed the same peal in parts, for the convenience of the caller, which peal, after being divided into parts, was (I believe) rung the first time by the Cumberlands, at Shoreditch, on the 12th October, 1754, and conducted by Mr. George Gross.

In the year 1752, it appears Mr. Holt left the Union Scholars and joined the Ancient Society of College Youths, and rang two peals with that company, with whom, it is supposed, he continued so long as he remained a practical ringer; it, however, may be remarked that Mr. Holt's name does not appear in any peal or performance of any kind with any society whatever after ringing the two peals above-mentioned with the Ancient Society of College Youths.

The Society appears (by the book) to have been in a prosperous state till about the year 1754, but in 1757 their last peal was rung, at which time the Society became extinct (or thereabouts) as most of the members' names about this latter date are to be found in the books of other societies. In the year 1754, Mr. Albion, an active member of this Company, and a celebrated writer of peals, appears to have left London to fulfil an appointment as master of a large school at Bath, where he continued to the year of his death, 1805, and when the Union Scholars became extinct, he, being the writer of the peals, the Peal Book was sent to him at Bath, as a present, with a request to keep it, which he did to the time of his decease, when the same was afterwards presented to one John Bush (a Bath ringer), for the Bath Abbey Company, which he kept, *as his own*, till his decease, in 1821. It was afterwards in the hands of others in Bath many years, in fact to the time I happened to visit Bath (while on a tour through the West of England), when it by chance was shewn to me, and to my astonishment I was asked "*the meaning*" of such a book! I soon discovered what it was and, after perusing it, made an offer and purchased it for 10s.; this was on the 2nd day of September, 1846. Upon calculation I discovered this book had been in Bath nearly 90 years, and was always supposed, by the London people, to have been for many years entirely lost or destroyed. Prior to Mr. Albion's leaving London for Bath, as before-mentioned, he wrote members' names and peals in the books of nearly every society in London, down to the time of his departure for Bath, viz.:—all the names and peals in the Ancient Society of College Youths' book from 17— to 1754; a few peals in the Eastern Scholars' book in 1752-3; all the peals from 1741 to 1754, and the whole of the names in the Union Scholars' book, and the members' names from 1747 to 1753 in the Cumberland's book. This fact is perceptible to anyone possessing a small portion of genuine discernment of ornamental writing. Thus Mr. Albion left London in 1754, and his name appears in a peal of Union Triples with the Bath Company on the 9th of December in that year, which peal he recorded in his usual ornamental style upon paper with his name signed as the writer thereof, which record was presented to me in December, 1846, by Mr. Albion, his only son (then 80 years of age), as a lover of ringing antiquities, the possession of which I retain to this day."

ADDITIONAL MANUSCRIPTS,

Vol. 13968, *page* 23.

Mr. Osborne also gives this account of the finding of this book:—

"The following history relates to the singular discovery of the Ancient Society of Union Scholars' *Peal Book*, which was supposed to have been lost or destroyed very many years since, but was perchance found and purchased by me, while on a visit to Bath, in December, 1846.—

Whereas, Mr. James Albion, a native of Hackney, Middlesex, born in or about the year 1727, by profession a mercantile clerk and professional writer, resided in London till the year 1753, when he went to live at Bath, and there opened a school, which he carried on with great reputation to the year 1805, the year of his death. During his time in London, he wrote all the last peals in the Union Scholars' Book, and when that Society became extinct (about the year 1757), this book was sent to him as a *present*, being the writer thereof—which he kept till his decease, when the same was presented to the Bath Abbey Ringers Society, by his only surviving son, James Albion—who made this statement to me in 1846, above-mentioned, and was then residing at No. 1, Chapel Court, in the City of Bath, in the 80th year of his age. This book was entrusted to the care of one John Bush,—a Bath ringer—to hand to his society—instead of which he kept it for himself to the time of his death, which event occurred in 1821, Afterwards it remained in the hands of different members of that society, as private property, till it was purchased by me on the 2nd day of December, 1846: At this period the book was in a very dilapidated state from age and illusage. I brought it to London in its original state, and afterwards took it to pieces, cleaned the whole of the leaves, mounted them upon new paper, and made all defects good about the writing, &c.—with a title page to the peals—there being no original—added some antique views of churches, with several other interesting and ancient performances, which do not appear elsewhere on paper, all of which have been collected and written by E. J. Osborne.

Upon perusal of the original leaves it will be perceived that Mr. Albion was (besides the writer) a ringing member of the Society of Union Scholars, and rang in nearly all the peals to the time of his leaving London for Bath. It will be also, afterwards, seen that he joined the Bath Ringing Company, and rang a peal of Union Tripples with that Company, which he recorded upon paper, and the same was presented to me by Mr. Albion (his son) in 1846, which I have placed for perusal at the end of these leaves, which originally formed the Society of Union Scholars Book—the subject of this address. E J. Osborne."

Additional Manuscripts Vol. 19371.

"THE

NAMES OF THE MEMBERS

OF THE

SOCIETY OF UNION SCHOLARS,

Commencing from the 1st of May in the year 1713:—

Stewards.	1713.	Masters.
1714	Wm: Hodges	1713
1713	Wm. Balding	1715
1713	Wm. Freeborn	1714
1714	Robt. French	
	Robt. Bawlwin	
	John Medley	
1715	Thos. Goodridge	
1715	Thos. Wright	
	1714.	
1716	Wm. Coster	1717
1716	Rd. Walker	1723
1717	Thos. Richards	1720
1717	Alex. White	1719
	1715.	
1722	Ed. Franks	1716
1718	Jno. Stiles	
1718	Rd. Willson	
	1716.	
1721	Thos. Perrin	
1719	Saml. Moss	1718
1719	Jno. Russell	
1720	Thos. Wheeler	
	Rd. Oswald	
1720	Wm. Strange	

Stewards.	1717.	Masters.
1720	Chas. Marsh	
1721	Edw. Archer	
	And. Williams	1721
	1718.	
1722	Danl. Steward	
	AmbroseTaylor	1722
	1719.	
1723	Robt. Stretch	
1723	Saml. How	1724
1724	Rd. Steel	1725
	1720.	
1724	Wm. Smithson	
	Jas. Field	
	1721.	
1743	W. Scarsbrook	1746
1725	Jno. Stanton	
1725	Wm. Smith	1726
	1722.	
1727	Hy. Macfarland	
1726	Jas. Mason	
1726	Wm. Howard	1727

Stewards.		Masters.
	1723.	
1727	Thos. Burnett	1728
1728	Geo. Hawdon	
	Wm. Gill	1729
1728	Richd. Quick	
	1724.	
	Jno. Salter	
1731	Thos. Fisher	
1731	Thos. Mead	
	1725.	
1730	Wm. Ayres	1731
1729	Jno. Flanders	1730
1729	Aron Dove	
	1726.	
1730	Wm. Killingsworth	1732
	Jno. Adams	
	1727.	
	Adam Children	
1732	Jno. Hodges	1733
1743	Saml. Slaughter	
	1728.	
	Chas. Kettleby	
1732	Jno. Jennings	
	1729.	
	Jas. Newcomb	
	Wm. Fenner	
	1730.	
1733	Andrew Stevens	
1733	Jno. Rawlins	
	1731.	
1734	Thos. Barrett	1735
1737	John Dobyns	1734
1737	Thos. Wetherly	
	Jas. Newby	
	1732.	
1742	Jos. Fielding	
1734	Wm. Young	1743
	1733.	
1737	Philip Barringer	
1741	Thos. Fletcher	
	1734.	
1736	Jos. Brown	
	Danl. Bigsby	
1735	Saml. Walton	1737
	Geo. Lawrence	
	1735.	
1735-39	Capt. R. Hill	1736
1736	Jno. Denmead	1738
	Thos. Palmer	
1737-46	Ed. Underwood	1740
	Fras. Popham, Esq.	
	Saml. Vaughan	
	1736.	
	Saml. Randall	
1738-39	Chas Spurt	
1738-39	Chas. Bride	
1738-39	Jno. Hopkins	
1738	Robt. Beard	
	1737.	
1740	Jno. Barker	
1744	Jas. Bohun	1739
1742	Jos. Matthews	1745
	1738.	
	Jno. Braly	
	Jos. Dickinson	
	Jno. Herrin	
	Jno Sharp	
	Philemon Mainwaring	

Stewards.		Masters.
	1739.	
	Jas Edwards	
	Wm. Simms	
	Jno. Blake	
	Jno. Dagley	
	1740.	
	Jos. Ashton	
	Wm. Lovell	
	1741.	
1740	Jas. Rodgers	1741
1741	Wm. Mason	1742
	1742.	
	Thos. Davis	
	Thos. James	
	1743.	
1744	Wm. Mattson	
	Robt. James	
	Jno. Scollough	1744
	1744.	
1745	Wm. Meddus	
1745-46	Jacob Hall	1747
	1745.	
	John Holt*	1749
	Hy. Young	
	1746.	
	Thos. Jones	
	Geo. Ware	
1747	Hy. Savory, Putney	1748
1747	Jno. Brown	
	1747.	
1748	Thos. Ward	
1748	Jas. Fawkes	
	Isaac Hannum	

Stewards.		Masters.
	1747.	
	Fras. Busshell	
	Thos. Vandyke	
	Jno. Lloyd	
	Jas. Albion	
	1748.	
	Thos. Jackson	
	Edw. Powell*	
	Jno. Jas. Short*	
	Jas. Marshall	
	1749.	
	Edw. Davis	
	Thos. Thomas	
	Edw. Thomas*	
	Jos. Jones	
	Jas. Davis	
	Jno. Lokes	
	1750.	
	Thos Fulford	
	H. Cowley, Twickenham	
	Robt. Fenn	
	Jno. Meredith	
	Phillip Thacker	
	Jno. Roames	
	P. Cowley, Twickenham	
	Rd. Cadman	
	Saml. Vains	
	Wm. Sharpe	
	Hy. Vestell	
	†Jas. Tichborne	
	Jas. Vickers	
	Hy. Penn	
	Hy. Cashbrook	
	Jno, Curtiss, Oxford	
	Mat. Ashley } Hillingdon, Middlesex	
	Wm. Smith } Hillingdon, Middlesex	
	Jno. Line } Hillingdon, Middlesex	

* Extra illuminated.

† Crossed out and X written in margin.

Stewards.	*1750.	Masters.	Stewards.	*1750.	Masters.
	Wm. Underwood			Wm. Cooper	
	Geo. Fleury			Wm. Kiddall	
	Jno. Barney, Bucks.			Hy. Lewis	
1754	Rd. Royce			Thos. Bowston	
1754	Rd. Millson			Wm. Blair	
	Jno. Jenner			Jno. Wheatley	
	Jno. Frasier			Matthew Lowns	
	Saml. Daniel			Barnaby Stanton	
	Jno. Goodspeed			Jno. Richards	
	Jno. Hayes			Chas. Powell	
	Thos. Milton			Thos. Nash	
	Jno.Cardwell		1757	Wm. Robinson	
	Wm. Richardson			Jno. Shatton	
	Jno Paddok			Wm. Mills	
	Jno. Smith			Wistanley Richardson	
	Jas. Keatt			Geo Carbery	
	Wm. Stephenson			Chas. Goffe	
	Thos. Storer		1757	Thos. Banks.	

* All the names after the year 1750 are entered under the same heading, but it is probable that these are the Members who joined the Society from 1750 to the time of its dissolution. In copying the names etc. from the original records, all mis-spelt names and words have been produced without alteration.

ORDERS TO BE OBSERVED BY THE SOCIETY OF UNION SCHOLARS.

IMPRIMIS. *It is Order'd,*

That on the first Monday in May yearly (being the year's peal) election be made of three members, one of whom to serve the office of Master and the other two the office of Stewards for the year ensuing, and upon refusal of such persons so elected, they shall forfeit five shillings to the use of the Company. N.B.—That election be made of a member to serve the office of Master according to his seniority.

Order'd:—

That the two persons so elected to officiate as Stewards together with the Master, determine such matters or things as shall be for the good and credit of the Company.

That no man be admitted except he is a civil man and a sufficient ringer. For approbation, he shall ring a bell with the Company, and if approved of, on his paying one shilling at his entry to the Warner shall be admitted by the Master at a publick meeting of the Company.

Order'd :—

That on the first Monday in May, yearly and every year, the Company meet together at such convenient time and in such place (within the City of London) as to them shall seem most proper, the Stewards to provide a Dinner, and in order to defray the charge of this Dinner, the Stewards shall receive of each member two shillings and sixpence, and for the better hindrance of excess it is further ordered that the year's forfeits be disbursed towards the overplus (if any such there be) of this expense. The Stewards to expend no more than any other member and—

It is unanimously agreed,

That a weekly peal be kept on every Monday, the time appointed for meeting is precisely at 7 o'clock in the winter and at 8 o'clock in the summer. N.B.—The placo of meeting not to be out of the City aforesaid.

Order'd:—

That at all such weekly meetings, each member expend sixpence and if the reckoning amounts to more the Stewards shall pay it.

That, if any of this Society being timely warned at any extraordinary meeting shall fail in his appearance, for such neglect shall pay sixpence, save on a very emergent occasion.

That as Gaming is considered a growing evil and tends manifestly to the Prejudice not only of this but of all other Societies—

Resolv'd therefore:—

Whosoever shall be found guilty thereof shall forfeit for the first offence one shilling, and if afterwards the Person so found guilty commits the same fault, he shall be expell'd the Society.

Order'd—

That since no Society, whether for Gain or Pleasure can well last without having due respect to the Divine Being, whereby 'tis presumed things may be better regulated for the reputation of this fraternity, it is

Resolv'd—

That if any Member at any Meeting of Ringing or other assembly shall curse, swear, or vainly utter the name of God whether it is owing to his Ebriety or any other unseemly Quality, for every such Fault shall pay twopence, and if by too frequent a practice of the same shall be deem'd a Corrupter and Expell'd the Society.

Order'd—

That the Stewards shall keep a brief Abstract of all Forfeits to the end, that they may be capable to Inform any one of his offence if Scrupled or Denied.

That the Company shall Elect a carefull honest Man to be their Warner, who, upon the Instructions given him by the Master or Stewards, shall give notice to such part of the Society so intended to meet, for the Execution of which office the Stewards shall collect one shilling per man throughout the Society, to be paid him on every Feast Day yearly.

That these Orders be in the Custody of the Master and shall be Read by him or his Order at the Entrance of any New Member, whereof, if he fail he shall pay one shilling.

And lastly, it is further *order'd, agreed and concluded upon,*

That if any Dispute should arise, touching or concerning these Orders or Rules or anything Therein contained, the matter so in dispute shall be referr'd to the Master and Stewards who shall Decide the same, and the person or persons concern'd not submitting to their Determination shall be Expell'd the Society."

(On the next page is a drawing of a Church, under which is written)

"A Perspective View of the Parish Church of St. Clement Danes in the Strand, most humbly inscrib'd to this Society by their most humble servt., James Albion."

THE FOLLOWING ARE

THE ORIGINAL PEALS

RUNG BY THE

SOCIETY OF UNION SCHOLARS,

Established the 1st *of May*, 1713.

(Full page illumination, beautifully executed in Mr. Osborne's handwriting.)

---

* No. 1. *September* 12*th*, 1718.

This Society rang at ST. DUNSTAN-IN-THE-EAST
the first true and compleat peal of

5040 HICK TREBLES.

Wm. Hodges	1	Richd. Oswald	5
Robt. French	2	Thos. Goodridge	6
Wm. Freeborn	3	Robt. Baldwin	7
Jn. Medley	4	Wm. Balding	8

---

* No. 2. *December* 27*th*, 1718.

This Society rang at ST. DUNSTAN-IN-THE-EAST
the first true and compleat peal of

5120 UNION BOB.

Jn. Medley	1	Richd. Oswald	5
Robt. French	2	Thos. Perrin	6
Wm. Freeborn	3	Robt. Bawld'g	7
Edwd. Franks	4	Wm. Balding	8

---

* See Appendix.

*No. 3. *February* 11*th*, 1736.

This Society rang at ST. MARTIN'S-IN-THE-FIELDS
the first true and compleat peal of

5040 TEN IN.

Call'd by Jno. Denmead.

Danl. Biggsby	1	Jos. Brown	6
Ed. Underwood	2	‡*Jno. Denmead*	7
Sam. Vaughan	3	Thos. Barrett	8
Thos. Palmer	4	Fra. Popham	9
Ralph Hill	5	Sam. Walton	10

---

*No. 4. *Thursday February* 24*th*, 1736.

This Society rang on the eight smallest bells at
ST. MARTIN'S-IN-THE-FIELDS
the first compleat peal of

5040 GRANDS'R TREBLES.

Prick't and call'd by Jno. Denmead.

Performed in 3 hours and 10 minutes, by

Edw. Underwood	Treble	Tho. Weatherly	5
Sam. Vaughan	2	Jno. Dunmead	6
Ralph Hill	3	Tho. Barrett	7
Geo. Lawrence	4	Sam. Walton	Tenor

No. 5. *March the* xx., mdccxxxvi.

The Society rang at ST. GILES'S-IN-THE-FEILDS
the first true and compleat peal of

5040 BOB MAJOR

ever performed on those bells, and performed in 3 hours 22 mins.

Call'd by Jno. Denmead.

W. Scarsbrook	Treble	R. Hill	5
L. Underwood	2	T. Barratt	6
S. Vaughan	3	J. Denmead	7
T. Weatherly	4	Jos. Brown	Tenor

---

* See Appendix.

‡ The name of the Conductor, here given in italics, is printed in red in the original.

*No. 6. *July the 25th*, 1736.

This Society rang at ST. GEORGE'S, SOUTHWARK, the first true and compleat peal of

5040 BOB MAJOR.

Call'd by Jn. Denmed.

Thos. Palmer	1	Thos. Barrett	5
Ed. Underwood	2	T. Weatherly	6
Ral. Hill	3	Jno. Denmed	7
Step. Picard	4	Sl. Vaugh'n	8

---

*No. 7. *February the 26th*, 1738.

This Society rang at ST. GILES'S-IN-THE-FEILDS the first true and compleat peal of

5040 HAM TREBLES.

perform'd in 3 hours 1 min.

Call'd by John Denm'd.

Jn. Jennings	Treble	Jam. Newby	5
Sam. Vaughan	2	Jn. Denmed	6
Ralph Hill	3	Sam Randall	7
Saml. Walton	4	Jas. Bohun	Tenor

No. 8. *May the* xx., mdccxxxviii.

This Society rang at ST. MARTIN'S-IN-THE-FEILDS the first true and compleat peal of

5040 BOB MAJOR TREBLES CONTAINING THE TREBLE LEADS AND BOBS OF YE COMPLEAT PEAL OF 40320 BOB MAJOR, EIGHT IN.

Prickt and called by Jn. Denmed.

Perform'd in 2 hours 55 mins.

Jos. Brown	Treble	Sam Walton	5
Jas. Bohun	2	Jn. Denmead	6
Ral. Hill	3	Sam Vaughan	7
Sam Newby	4	Chas. Spurll	Tenor

---

* See Appendix.

No. 9. *Monday, February the* 19*th*, 1738-9.

This Society rang at ST. SAVIOUR, SOUTHWARK, the first true and compleat peal of

5040 BOB MAJOR ROYAL, OTHERWISE TEN IN

ever performed on those bells.

It was compleated in 4 hours 10 mins., by ye ten following persons :—

JN. BRALEY	Treble	GEO. LAURANCE	6
JOS. DICKENSON	2	CHAS. SPURLL	7
WM. SCARSBROOK	3	SAM WALTON	8
RALPH HILL	4	JNO. HOPKINS	9
JNO. DENMED	5	PHILEN MAINWARING	Tenor

Call'd by Jno. Denmead.

N.B.—The Tenor, 51c: 2: 7.

No. 10. *July the* 29*th*, 1739.

This Society rang att ST. MARY'S, LAMBETH, in 3 hours 10 mins., a true and compleat peal of

5040 BOB MAJOR. EIGHT IN.

JNO. HERING	Treble	WM. SIMMS	5
JOS. DICKENSON	2	JNO. BLAKE	6
JNO. SHARP	3	JNO. DAGLEY	7
JAS. EDWARDS	4	PHILE WAINWARING	Tenor

No. 11. ALL SAINTS, FULHAM.

The Society on *the* 23*rd day of November*, 1741, rang compleatly in 3 hours and 18 mins.,

5264 BOB MAJOR.

The performers were—

JOS. ASHTON	1	W. LOVELL	5
JNO. DAGLEY	2	JOS. DICKENSON	6
JNO. HERRIN	3	WM. SIMMS	7
JNO. SHARP	4	JAS. BOHUN	8

*No. 12. ST. MARGARET'S, Westminster.

The Society rang on the 27*th October*, 1747, a compleat peal of

5040 BOB MAJOR,

and was performed in 3 hrs. 20 mins., by—

Jno. Holt	Treble	John Lloyd	5
Jas Bohun	2	Thos. Ward	6
Geo. Ware	3	Jas. Newby	7
Jacob Hall	4	Robt. James	Tenor

The first Treble lead		The Course ends‡	
21436587		6423578	—
24163857		2654378	
42618375		5236478	
46281735		4352678	—
64827153		6543278	—
68472513		4625378	
86745231		2436578	
87654321	In this Peal the 6th	5324678	—
78563412	is at home 12 times.	2563478	
75836142		6245378	
57381624		3462578	—
53718264		5634278	—
35172846		2356478	—
31527486		4523678	—
13254768		3425678	
13527486			
At a bob 4ths place.		of the first 1680.	

N.B—Call'd by John Holt.

* See Appendix.

‡ The course ends, followed by a mark (—), are written in red.

*No. 13. ST. GILES'S-IN-THE-FEILDS.

The Society rang on the 1st *day of November*, in the year 1747, a compleat peal of

5040 BOB MAJOR,

and in 3 hrs. and 3 mins,,

by the following persons ye same was performed:—

Walter Harvey	Treble	John Holt	5
Jas. Fawkes	2	Jno. Lloyd	6
Jacob Hall	3	Robt. James	7
Thos. Ward	4	Jas. Bohun	Tenor

16423857		13647285	,,
14357682		15243867	,,
12654837		12367584	,,
16437285		14562837	,,
15236847		16452837	,,
12647583		14237685	,,
13542367	These are the bobs	15634827	,,
15267381	of the first 1680.	16427583	,,
14365827		13526847	,,
16435827		15647382	,,
14527683		12345867	,,
13624857		13567284	,,
16457382		14263857	,,
12356847		14235678	,,

Call'd by John Holt.

---

* See Appendix

*No. 14. ST. MARTIN'S-IN-THE-FEILDS.

On the 9th day of December, 1748,

a compleat peal of

5040 BOB MAJOR

was rang by the Society on the eight smallest bells,

which peal was performed by the persons following, viz:—

Je. Hannum	Treble	Saml. Green	5
Thos. Vandyke	2	Stn. Pickhaver	6
Jno. Holt	3	Rt. Mortimer	6
Ed. Powell	4	Geo. Ware	Tenor

The bobs at the course ends of the first 1680.

16423578
15264378
13652478
12453678
16524378
13265478
14632578
12534678
16325478
14263578
15642378

The bobs of this peal were call'd by Jno. Holt.

The treble leads

12357486
13728564
17836245
18674352
16485723
16452837
16423578

of the first course.

---

* See Appendix.

*No. 15 ST. MARGARET'S, Westminster.

On the 9th of July, 1749,

was rang by this Society a compleat peal of

6000 BOB MAJOR,

in 4 hrs. and 8 mins. the same was performed,

John Holt	Treble	and the Performers were,	Edward Powell	5
Thos. Ward	2		Robert Mortimer	6
Jacob Hall	3		John Lloyd	7
James Newby	3		Step. Pickhaver	Tenor

12357486		14352678	—‡
12378564		12453678	
18645372		15324678	—
18657423	This peal was never	14523678	
16723845	rang before and is	13425678	
18267534	exactly 6000.	12534678	—
18273645	Compos'd and call'd	13254678	—
12345867	by John Holt.	15432678	—
12356478		13542678	—
12367584		12345678	
14562837			
The bobs of the 1st 25 leads.		These are the 560 ends.	

---

* See Appendix.

‡ The course ends followed by a — are written in red.

*No. 16. ST. MARTIN'S-IN-THE-FIELDS.

The Society *on the 8th of August,* 1749 rang a compleat peal of

5040 PLAIN BOB TREBLES

on the eight smallest bells, and the same was performed in 3 hours and 20 mins. by—

Robt. James	Treble	Jacob Hall	5
Jno. Holt	2	Rt. Mortimer	6
Jno. Lloyd	3	Edw. Powell	7
Geo. Meakins	4	Jno. James	Tenor

Call'd by John Holt.

The first Treble lead.	The Bobs of
2143657	1235746
2416375	1645273
4261735	1642357
4627153	1526473
6472513	1652473
6745231	1543762
7654321	1354762
7563412	1643527
5736142	1645732
5371624	1235674
3517264	1236457
3152746	1562374
1325476	1256374
1352746	1534726
At a bob 4ths place.	1453726
	the first 840.

* See Appendix.

*No. 17. CHRIST CHURCH, Surrey,

October the 15th, 1749.

A compleat peal of

5040 BOB MAJOR

was by the Society rang, and in 3 hours and 15 mins.,

the same was perform'd by the following persons, viz:—

Oliver Ellingsworth	Treble	Step. Peckhaver	5
Jacob Hall	2	Jno. Holt	6
Saml. Green	3	Jno. Lloyd	7
Rt. Mortimer	4	Thos. Prior	Tenor

16423857		15236478
12643857		15267384
16357284		14365827
15637284		16435827
12356478	These are the bobs of	13645827
12367584	the first 1680.	16527384
14562837	Call[d] by John Holt.	12657384
16452837		13526478
15642837		13567284
16237584		14263857
13627584		14235678

* See Appendix.

*No. 18. ST. SEPULCHRE'S, London.

On the 5th of December, 1749,

was rung by the Society on the eight largest bells, a compleat peal of

5040 BOB MAJOR,

and in 3 hours and 45 mins, it was performed by—

Jas. Albion	Treble	Geo. Helliwell	5
Jacob Hall	2	Thos. Ward	6
Jas. Newby	3	Jno. Lloyd	7
Jno. Holt	4	Thos. Prior	Tenor

These are the bobs of the 1st 560.

12357486		12534678	—‡
16452837		13425678	
16423578		13254678	—
16437285		13542678	—
15236847	N.B.—This is the	14235678	
15264378	first peal of Bob	14352678	—
15247683	Major ever rang	14523678	—
13645827	on the New	12345678	
13652478	Bells.		
13627584	Call'd by John Holt.		
14523867			
15367482			
12465837			
12453678		(The 560 ends of the Peal.)	

---

* See Appendix.

‡ The course ends followed by a — are written in red.

*No. 19. ST. BRIDGET'S *alias* ST. BRIDE'S, LONDON.

The Society *on the* 16*th of March* 1749 / 1750, rang on the eight smallest bells in this steeple a compleat peal of

5056 BOB MAJOR.

and in 2 hrs. and 57 mins. it was performed by the persons following:

JAS. ALBION	Treble	SAML. GREEN	5
WALTER HARVEY	2	JACOB HALL	6
JAS. NEWBY	3	JNO LOKES	7
JNO. HOLT	4	THOS' WARD	Tenor

17864523	12654837		13657482	12567483
2356478	6437285		4536278	3462857
2367584	3647285		4567382	6342857
6237584	2436578		2364857	4632857
3627584	2467385		6234857	6257483
5236478	5362847		3624857	5627483
5267384	5324678	These are the bob	6457382	4256378
4365827	6253847	changes of the	5647382	4267583
4352678	5623847	peal.	3456278	3564827
6543827	6347582		3467582	3542678
4653827	4637582	Call'd by	2563847	6435827
6327485	5346278	John Holt.	2534678	3645827
2637485	5367482		6325847	6527384
4326578	2465837		2635847	2657384
4367285	6245837		6547283	3526478
5264837	4625837		4657283	3567284
16524837	16537482		12546378	14263857

* See Appendix.

*No. 20. ST. MARGARET'S, Westminster,

July 8*th*, 1750,

was rang by the Society a compleat peal of

5040 DOUBLE BOB MAJOR,

otherwise Double Eight in.

and in 3 hours 28 mins., it was perform'd by—

Jas. Albion	Treble	Thos. Ward	5
Jno. Holt	2	Jas, Tichborne	6
Rt. Buttersworth	3	Rt. Mortimer	7
Jno. Lloyd	4	Edw. Thomas	Tenor

21436587		43652	65324
24163857		56234	35426
42618375	Call'd by	23564—	45623
46281735	Jno. Holt.	62534	26354
64827153	‡Course ends of	52436	35264—
68472513	the 1st 1680.	42635	63254
86745231		36524	42356—
68472531		52364—	
86745213			
87654123			
78561432			
75816342			
57183624			
51738264			
15372846			
15738264			

* See Appendix.

‡ The course ends marked with a — are written in red.

*No. 21. St. GEORGE'S, Southwark.

The 9th of September, 1750.

The Society rang in 3 hours and 15 mins., a compleat peal of

5040 PLAIN BOB TREBLES.

The performers were as follows :—

Oliver Ellingsworth,	Treble	James Albion	5
John Holt	2	Edward Thomas	6
Thomas Ward	3	John Lloyd	7
Thomas Jackson	4	James Davis	Tenor

The first lead.		The Bobs.
2143657		1235746
2416375		645273
4261735		642357
4627153		526473
6472513		652473
6745231		543762
7654321	Call'd by John Holt.	354762
7563412		643527
5736142		645732
5371624		235674
3517264		236457
3152746		562374
1325476		256374
1352746		534726
		453726
		of the first 840.

* See Appendix.

*No. 22. St. GEORGE'S, Southwark.

The Society on *Sunday, January the 20th*, 1750, rang a compleat peal of

5040 BOB MAJOR.

and in 3 hrs. 24 mins. it was perform'd by the persons following :

46325			26354
64352			34256
32654			43265
23645			25463
65243	James Davis	Treble	52436
56234	John Holt	2	46253
24536	Jacob Hall	3	64235
42563	James Vickers	4	25634
53462	James Newby	5	52643
35426	Oliver Ellingworth	6	63542
46532	Thomas Ward	7	36524
64523	Jas. Tichborne	Tenor.	54326
53624			45362
35642			32465
62345			34256

The above Changes are the course ends of the 1st 1680.

The Bobs of this peal were call'd by Thomas Ward.

* See Appendix.

*No. 23. St. SEPULCHRE'S, London,

January 28*th*, 1750.

The Society in 3 hours and 42 mins. rang a compleat peal of

5094 GRANDSIRE CATORS,

being the first ever performed in that method on these bells

The performers were :—

Matthew Blackmore,	Treble	James Newby	6
Thomas Ward	2	James Vickers	7
John Holt	3	Oliver Ellingsworth	8
Thomas Jackson	4	Edward Werden	9
John Lloyd	5	James Davis	Tenor

213547698
231456789
324165879
342618597
436281957
463829175
648392715
684937251
869473521
896745312
987654132
978561423
795816243
759182634
571928364
517293846
152739486
125374968

At the end of the last course instead of once, 8.9 tis' once the 7th with the 8th.

75293846
46738295

These are extraordinary

65347289
32567489
54237689
35492867

Course ends.

78369254
39785642
75394826
89765234
26849375

These are extraordinary Bobs that were called to bring the bells round.

Call'd by John Holt.

This is the 1st Treble lead of the peal, which peal is divided into 4 courses and the Bobs of each course is called as follows :—

Once the 7th behind without the 8th, twice 7.8 twice 8.9 twice 7.8 twice 8.9 twice 7.8 once 8.9.

---

* See Appendix.

No. 24. St. MARTIN'S-IN-THE-FIELDS

Tuesday, February 19*th*, 1750.

The company rang on the ten largest bells a compleat peal of

5112 GRANDSIRE CATERS,

and in 3 hours 47 mins.

t'was performed by the following persons:—

Daniel Bigsby	1	James Tichborne	6
Jacob Hall	2	James Newby	7
John Holt	3	Oliver Ellingsworth	8
Joseph Dickenson	4	John Lloyd	9
Thomas Ward	5	James Davis	10

95384726	89765234
78965234	26849375

This peal was call'd as the former, except the above changes, which are bobs that were called to bring the bells round.

Call'd by John Hall.

---

*No. 25. St. MARGARET'S, Westminster.

March 14*th*, 1750.

The Society rang compleatly

5120 UNION BOB,

in 3 hours and 37 mins, it was performed by—

BOB CHANGES					OF THE FIRST COURSE.
7864523	James Albion	1	Oliver Ellingsworth	5	4237685
7842635	Jacob Hall	2	Thomas Ward	6	3427685
7823456	James Newby	3	John Lloyd	7	6234578
7835264	John Holt	4	Joseph Dickenson	8	3624578

The bobs call'd by John Holt.

These are the	course ends of the peal.
6532478	4256378
5463278	2345678

* For the calling of this peal see Appendix.

*No. 26. St. MARY'S, Hillingdon, Middlesex.

The Company on *Tuesday, the 9th of April*, 1751, rang a compleat peal of

5040 BOB MAJOR,

which peal was performed in 3 hours and 30 mins., by the persons whose names are particularly underwritten :—

James Davis	1	James Vickers	5
Thomas Jackson	2	James Newby	6
John Holt	3	Thomas Ward	7
James Albion	4	Joseph Dickenson	8

The bobs call'd by John Holt.

23564	35264	42563	25463	34562	45362
52364	42356	54263	34256	53462	23456

These are the bob changes at the course end.

[This peal was completed immediately after ringing 5800 Double Bob Major, the whole time being 7 hours 30 mins.]†

No. 28. St. MARY'S, Hillingdon Middlesex.

On Monday, August yᵉ 26th, 1751,

The Society rang in 3 hours and 25 mins., the first true and compleat‡ peal of

5040 DOUBLE BOB MAJOR,

(with the sixth at home, and in the tittum course twelve times each, which was performed by the following persons :—

John Holt	1	James Albion	5
Jacob Hall	2	James Vickers	6
Thomas Jackson	3	James Tichbourne	7
James Newby	4	John Lloyd	8

Compos'd and call'd by John Holt.

---

* See Appendix.

† There is nothing to certify that this peal of Double Bob Major was rung by the same company, but it seems most probable, as the time shews that it must have been rung without a stand. It was evidently, although such scanty particulars are given, reckoned by the Society as a performance, because the next peal is numbered 28, leaving Nos. 26 and 27 for these two performances.

‡ As the previous performance embraced a peal of Double Bob Major, it will be seen that it is not here claimed that this was the "*first* true and compleat peal" ever rang, but that it was the first of 5040 with the sixth twelve times each way. Unfortunately, some of these old records are very indefinitely worded, and when claiming to have rung the first peal in a certain method on the bells, if taken literally, the claim would be for the first performance in the method.

*No. 29. ST. BRIDGET'S, *otherwise* ST. BRIDE'S.

The Society *on the 20th of October*, 1751, rang a compleat peal of

5104 GRANDSIRE CINQUES,

and in 3 hours and 40 mins.

it was performed by the following persons:—

James Davis	1	James Albion	7
Wm. Underwood	2	James Vickers	8
John Lloyd	3	James Tichborne	9
James Newby	4	John Holt	10
Jacob Hall	5	Robert James	11
Thomas Jackson	6	George Fleury	12

Compos'd and call'd by John Holt.

No. 30. ALL-HALLOW'S Chipping Wycomb,

in the County of Bucks.

The Company *on Saturday, December 28th*, 1751, rang completely in 3 hours and 29 mins. a complete peal of

5040 PLAIN BOB TREBLES,

being the first hitherto ever rang on those bells.

The performers were:—

John Holt	1	James Newby	5
Thomas Jackson	2	James Vickers	6
James Albion	3	John Lloyd	7
Oliver Ellingsworth	4	George Fleury and James Davis	8

Call'd by John Holt.

---

* This record is surmounted with a drawing of a bell, a scroll, on which is pricked the first lead of bob singles, and a pile of books, on the back of one of these is written "——'s Art of Ringing"—unfortunately, by design, some one has cut out the name of the author.

No. 31. ST. MARGARET'S, WESTMINSTER,

February 16*th*, 1752.

The Society rang completely in 3 hours and 35 mins.,

a true and complete peal of

5040 COURT BOB.

being the first that was ever rang on those bells.

The performers were—

JAMES DAVIS	1	OLIVER ELLINGSWORTH	5
WM. UNDERWOOD	2	JAMES VICKERS	6
JOHN HOLT	3	JAMES NEWBY	7
JAMES ALBION	4	JOHN LLOYD	8

Call'd by John Holt.

No. 32. ST. GILES'S-IN-THE-FIELDS.

New style.

September the 25*th*, 1752.

The Society rang completely a peal of

5040 PLAIN BOB TREBLES.

in 3 hours 10 mins.

It was performed by the following persons, viz:—

JAMES DAVIS	1	ROBERT JAMES	5
JAMES VICKERS	2	WM. SMITH	6
JAMES NEWBY	3	JAMES TICHBOURNE	7
JOHN HOLT	4	GEORGE FLEURY	8

Call'd by John Holt.

No. 33. ST. ALPHANES, East Greenwich,

in the County of Kent.

The Company *on Sunday, March* 18*th*, 1753,

rang a complete peal of

5166 GRANDSIRE CATERS.

and in 3 hours and 40 mins.,

it was performed by the following persons, viz:—

George Fleury	1	James Tichborne	6
Isaac Hannum	2	James Newby	7
James Albion	3	Henry Young	8
Richard Royce	4	Samuel Muggeridge	9
John Clark	5	James Davis	10

The bobs of this peal were call'd by James Newby.

No. 34. ALL SAINT'S, Fullham.

The Company rang *on Tuesday, March* 12*th*, 1754, a complete peal of

5040 BOB MAJOR.

and in 3 hours 15 mins. it was performed by the following, viz:—

Daniel Bigsby	1	Thomas Jones	5	
Richard Oswald	2	Robert James	6	
Walt Harvey	3	James Tichborne	7	Call'd Bobs.
John Clark	4	James Davis	8	

No. 35. ST. MARY'S, HILLINGDON, in Middlesex.

The Society *on Monday, April* 15*th*, 1754, rung completely a fine peal of

5040 BOB MAJOR.

and in 3 hours and 33 mins.,

it was performed by the following persons :—

James Vickers	1	Richard Millson	5
John Frazier	2	Richard Royce	6
Robert James	3	John Jennett	7
James Davis	4	Samuel Daniel	8

James Vickers call'd the bobs.

No. 36. At ST. GILES'S IN THE FIELDS.

On Sunday, December 18*th*, 1757,

This Society rang compleatly, in 3 hours 16 mins. a true peal of

5040 GRANDSIRE TREBLES.

with singles, one at the end of each half, and each half divided into five courses, as it was compos'd by John Holt.

The performers were :—

Barnaby Stanton	1	Wm. Richardson	5
Wm. Nash	2	Thomas Nash	6
Walter Harvey	3	Thomas Jackson	7
Thomas Dalmer	4	Wm. Robinson	8

Call'd by Thomas Jackson."

Between the leaves of the peal book on which are recorded the peals Nos. 25 and 26 Mr. Osborne has inserted a copy of the tablet in St. Margaret's, Westminster, which commemorates the ringing of Holt's one part peal. This copy and Mr. Osborne's remarks thereon are here given

" *Sunday, July 7th,* 1751.

The Society of Union Scholars rang in this steeple with two singles,

the first true and complete peal of

5040 GRANDSIRE TRIPPLES.

which peal was performed in 3 hours and 15 minutes by the following persons :—

JAMES DAVIS	Treble	JAMES VICKERS	5
JAMES ALBION	2	JAMES NEWBY	6
JACOB HALL	3	JOHN LLOYD	7
THOMAS JACKSON	4	GEO. FLEURY & ED. DAVIS	tenor

The peal was composed and call'd by John Holt.

Captain Nicholas Spencer, and Mr. William Goff, } Churchwardens."

"The above is a copy and account of Mr. Holt's original one course peal of grandsire tripples which was rang by the Union Scholars as above described, vide *Clavis Campanalogia*, p.p. 56 and 57. This peal was not inserted in that Society's book with their other peals by reason as (I suppose) it was considered irregular for the conductor to call and not ring at the same time in the usual way,—therefore I have copied the tablet representing that achievement and have placed it here for perusal as being one of the principal performances rung by that Society.—E. J. O."

At the end of the book is the leaf whereon Mr. Albion recorded the peal which he performed with the Bath ringers, and which Mr. Osborne alludes to when relating the events that led to the discovery of this book. The drawing is surmounted by a bell on which is written "*Campanæ Sonans canore.*" The following is the record:—

"ST. JAMES, BATH.

The following changes are the back stroke leads of a true and complete peal of

5040 UNION TRIPPLES.

as 'twas rang by the

Bath Society, on Monday, December 9th, 1754,
and in 3 hours it was performed by the persons underwritten:—

JAMES ALBION	1	MARTIN DIBBLE	5
THOS. TAYLOR	2	JNO. LUCAS (call'd bobs)	6
RICHD- SANSDOWN	3	ANTHONY MORLEY	7
ISAAC SIMS	4	JNO. JMITH	8

James Albion, Scrip. et delt., 1760."

(Then follows a peal of union tripples by the treble leads.)

APPENDIX.

——:o:——

Mr. Osborne having at length described tho doings of this Society, we purpose therefore only to make mention of such points of interest as may suggest themselves in connection with the different ringing performances of the Union Scholars.

No. 1. In the note book of Benjamin Annable, now in the possession of one of the writers, there is a method called "Gawthorne's Hic Triples," which is Grandsire with third and fifth place bobs, the "Hic" being used to denote the latter call. We therefore consider that there can be little doubt that this was a Grandsire peal of this description; whether however it was Garthon's original peal there is no means of ascertaining, still we think the evidence points to this conclusion. In Annable's book the ordinary method of Union Triples is given under the heading of "Baldwin's Union Triples," this gives strong confirmation to the Hick Triples being Grandsire with fifth place bobs, as in all probability the author of "Union Triples" was the same Robert Baldwin who rang the seventh in this and the following peal, and from his presumed abilities and his station at the seventh we may not be considered rash if we point to the probability of his having conducted both peals.

No. 2. Although the calling of this peal is not given in the peal book, it has been handed down to us and so far back as 1788, it is stated in *the Clavis* that the annexed peal is the one here recorded. Perhaps however the most curious fact is the statement of the authors of *the Clavis* that it was not until fifty years after the time when this peal was rung that the discovery was made of the necessity of further proof than the truth of the treble leads in this method, which it is perhaps hardly necessary to state is that now known as Oxford Treble Bob Major.

5120	B.	W.	H.
35264	-		
56342	-		
64523	-		
36245	-	2	2

Four times repeated.

No. 3. As the first peal of Bob Royal was the one rung by the College Youths at St. Bride's, on November 22nd, 1725, it is probable that the real meaning of this very decided claim to the *first* peal is only to be taken to signify that this was the first on the bells or by the Society. All these ancient records are very indefinite in such matters.

No. 4. This is one of the unexplained mysteries connected with the statement so tenaciously adhered to by some persons that the *first* peal of Grandsire Triples was not performed until 1751.

No. 6. This is another example of the very indefinite manner in which these peals are recorded.

No. 7. Mr. Osborne, in an M.S. copy of this peal, calls them " Hack Trebles " still, although we have every reason to read it " Hick," we consider " Ham" nearer the mark, though the style of illumination adopted in this word renders the correct reading decidedly obscure.

Nos. 12 to 14. No. 12 is the first peal in which John Holt (who joined the Society in 1745) took part. No. 13 is Annable's well known peal, and No. 14 is a musical example on the five course plan with the fewest omits possible. The calling of these Bob Major peals by the usual course end plan is annexed.

No. 12.

5040	M.	W.	H.
64235	-	-	-
26543	-	-	
52364	-	-	
43526	-	-	-
65432	-	-	-
46253	-	-	
24365	-	-	
53246	-	-	-
25634	-	-	
62453	-	-	
34625	-	-	-
56342	-	-	-
23564	-	-	-
45236	-	-	-
34256	-		

Twice repeated.

J. Holt.

No. 13.

5040	W.	M.	H.
43652		-	
64235	-	-	
26543	-	-	
52364	-	-	
35426	-	-	
——			
45623		-	
64352	-	.	
36245	-	-	
23564	-	-	
52436	-	-	
——			
42635	-	-	
64523	-	-	
56342	-	-	
35264	-	-	
42356	-	-	-

Twice repeated.

B. Annable.

No. 14.

5040	W.	M.	H.
64235	-	-	-
52643	-	-	-
36524	-	-	-
53462	-	-	
24536	-	-	-
——			
65243	-	-	-
32654	-	-	-
46325	-	-	-
34562	-	-	
25346	-	-	-
——			
63254	-	-	-
42635	-	-	-
56423	-	-	-
45362	-	-	
34256	-	-	

Twice repeated.

J. Holt.

No. 15. This composition is not very easy to understand by the course ends, &c., given in the record, as there are several ways by which the same 560 ends can be brought up. Mr. H. Hubbard has kindly elucidated the matter by shewing that as the wrong and middle are called in every course, the following peal is very easily perceived to be the correct one.

These are the bob changes of the first 25 leads:—

2357486
2378564
8645372
8657423
6723845
8267534
8273645
2345867
2356478
2367584
4562837

This gives the course end 52436, after which the peal runs in five course parts, thus :

	W.	M.	H.	(continued)	W.	M.	H.
45623	-	-		23645	-	-	
64352	-	-		62534	-	-	
36245	-	-		56423	-	-	
52364	-	-	-	34562	-	-	-
43526	-	-	-	25346	-	-	-
54632	-	-		32654	-	-	
65243	-	-		63425	-	-	
26354	-	-		46532	-	-	
43265	-	-	-	54263	-	-	
24536	-	-		32546	-	-	-
52643	-	-		53624	-	-	
65324	-	-		65432	-	-	
36452	-	-		46253	-	-	
24365	-	-	-	32465	-	-	-
53246	-	-	-	54326	-	-	-
25634	-	-		35642	-	-	
62453	-	-		63254	-	-	
46325	-	-		26435	-	-	
53462	-	-	-	42563	-	-	
45236	-	-		35426	-	-	-
24653	-	-		43652	-	-	
62345	-	-		64235	-	-	
36524	-	-		26543	-	-	
45362	-	-	-	35264	-	-	-
34256	-	-		23456	-	-	

No. 16. Is an interesting peal of Bob Triples in like halves, with a single at the half peal ends as given below on the left. The curious feature of this peal is that it is the foundation of the peal of Holt's without a single, as after the course end 23645, he subsequently interpolated the following part, which then ran on from the course end 63542 as this peal and became a peal without a single in three parts. This peal is given in *the Clavis.*

23456	M.	W.	H.
64235	-	-	-
24536		-	
54632		-	
35642	-		
64352	-		-
23645	-	-	-
63542		-	
53246		-	
45236	-		
34256	:		

Five times repeated with the addition of singles at the half peal ends.

J. Holt.

	23645	M.	W.	H.
Out	35246			
	43256	-		
	24635	-	-	
	64532		-	
	54236		-	
Fourths	42536	-	-	
	52634		-	
	35624	-		
	23654	-		
	62435	-	-	
In	63542		-	

By introducing this part into the foregoing peal it runs the extent without singles in three parts.

No. 17.

No. 17. This is a 5040 of Bob Major the given part of which is to be twice repeated.

No. 18. Is called in the same way as No. 14.

23456	W.	M.	H.
43652		- -	
63254		-	
56234	-		
23564	-		-
52436	-	-	
42635		-	
62534		-	
36524	-		
52364	-		-
35426	-	-	
45623		-	
65324		-	
26354	-		
35264	-		-
42356	-	-	-

No. 19. 5056 Bob Major. An interesting production which runs by the course ends thus :—

	W.	M.	H.	(continued)	W.	M.	H.	(continued)	W.	M.	H.
23564			-	53624		-		24653		-	
62534	-			63425		-		64352		-	
36524	-			26435	-			56342	-		
52364	-		-	43265	-		-	34562	-		-
43526	-	-	-	24536	-	-		25346	-	-	-
				54632		-		35642		-	
				64235		-		65243		-	
				36245	-			46253	-		
				24365	-		-	25463	-		-
				53246	-	-	-	42356	-	-	
				23645		-		32654		-	
				63542		-		62453		-	
				46532	-			56423	-		
				53462	-		-	42563	-		-
				45236	-	-		35426	-	-	-
				25634		-		45623		-	
				65432		-		65324		-	
				36452	-			26354	-		
				45362	-		-	35264	-		-
				34256	-	-		23456	-	-	

There is a Bob before in the first course.

J. Holt.

Nos. 20, 21, and 22. Nos. 20 and 22 are both Bob Major peals of 5040 changes, the first being in the Double, and the latter in the Single method, with regard to this peal it may be remarked that it is the only one in which John Holt rang that he did not also conduct, and also that it can hardly be called an original peal as it is simply Annable's peal with a bob at each course end where Annable has an omit. No. 21 is the peal of Bob Triples, the calling of which is given under No. 16.

No. 20. M. W. H.

	M.	W.	H.
43652	-		
56234	-	-	
23564		-	-
62534		-	
52436	-		
42635	-		
36524	-	-	
52364		-	-
65324		-	
35426		-	
45623	-		
26354	-	-	
35264		-	-
63254		-	
42356	-		-

No. 22. W. M. H.

	W.	M.	H.
64352		-	-
23645	-	-	-
56234	-	-	-
42563	-	-	-
35426	-	-	-
64523		-	-
35642	-	-	-
26354	-	-	-
43265	-	-	-
52436	-	-	-
64235		-	-
52643	-	-	-
36524	-	-	-
45362	-	-	-
34256	-	-	

Each of these parts to be twice repeated.

J. Holt.

No. 23. 5094 Grandsire Caters.

75293846
46738295

52493867	24695837	46392857	63594827
43526 78	65243	32465	54632
35426 78	52643	24365	46532
45623 89	62345	34562	56234
65324 89	32546	54263	26435
53624 78	25346	42563	64235
36524 78	53246	25463	42635
56423 89	23645	45362	62534
46325 89	63542	35264	52436
63425 78	35642	52364	24536
34625 78	56342	23564	45236
65347289	32567489	54237689	35492867
			78369254
			39785642
			75394826
			89765234
			26849375

J. Holt.

No. 24. Is 5112 of Grandsire Caters, called exactly in the same manner as the preceding peal, only from the bob change 35492867, the following bobs are called to bring it round, and the peal is improved as there are fewer changes after the tittum position.

35492867

95384726
78965234
89765234
26849375

No. 25. The calling of this peal is given with our remarks under peal No. 2.

No. 26. This peal is the same as No. 17.

The above peal is the last of which the calling is given, and curiously the next peal rung by the Society was Holt's one-part peal, as recorded at the end of the book by Mr. Osborne. During the few last years one of the writers has brought to light certain matters connected with the early peals of Grandsire Triples, which have promoted some discussion upon the subject and persons interested in this matter will not fail to observe the fact that even Mr. Holt's own Society, of which he was evidently the moving spirit,—having taken part in every peal rung by the Society since his first connection with it,—even this company cannot but we think have been prejudiced against it in some way, as they would not even insert its performance in their peal book. Whether this was, as Mr. Osborne surmises, because they considered it irregular for the conductor not to ring in the peal, or whether from some objection to the composition itself, is doubtful, but the fact nevertheless is strong evidence in favour of the theory that the restrictions then placed on Grandsire compositions, precluded the use of any other calls than ordinary bobs. It will also be noticed that Mr. Holt did not at *once* sever his connection with the Society, but that he rang five peals with them after this occurrence, it cannot therefore be taken for granted that it *was* owing to this incident that he went over to the College Youths. Many points for consideration in connection with this and other matters will present themselves to the careful reader, who we hope will not fail to be interested in these curious records of the early days of change ringing.

JASPER W. SNOWDON.
ROBERT TUKE.

ILKLEY, APRIL, 1877.

www.ingramcontent.com/pod-product-compliance
Lightning Source LLC
Chambersburg PA
CBHW031812090426
42739CB00008B/1247

9783337249786